CHRISTIAN MARRIAGE ETIQUETTE

12 Tips to Help Restore and Bring Balance to Your Marriage

By Gloria Duckett

CHRISTIAN MARRIAGE ETIQUETTE

EDITOR
Libra P. Green

CONTRIBUTING WRITER
Sole to Soul Publishing House, LLC

PUBLISHER & BOOK COACH
Dr Inga International
www.dringaintl.com

CREATIVE & MARKETING DESIGN
The Creativity Bar
www.thecreativitybar.com

ISBN#: 979-8-9850880-1-4

Copyright @ 2022, All rights reserved. No portion of this book may be reproduced, stored in a retrieval system, or transmittal in any form or by any means--electronic, mechanical, photocopy, recording, scanning, or other-- except for brief quotations in critical reviews or articles, without the prior written permission from the author.

Unless otherwise indicated, all Scripture quotations are taken from the King James Version of the Bible.

Printed in the USA

ABOUT THE AUTHOR

Gloria Duckett currently lives and has resided in Grand Prairie, Texas with her wonderful husband, Dwayne for over four decades. They have three adult children, eight grandchildren, and one great-granddaughter. They both attend and serve as Deacons at Bridge Builders International Church in Arlington, TX, under the leadership of Dr. Johnasen L. Pack. She is CEO of Mrs. Gloria's Family Childcare and Mrs. G's Teacakes & Goodies. She obtained her Associate's degree in Psychology from the University of Phoenix in 2011 and her undergraduate certificate in Business Management from Ashworth College in April 2020. She recently received her Bachelor's in Christian Counseling from the International College of Ministry.

When she is not working her businesses, she spends her time writing poetry, scribing, or journaling notes during church services. All in all, she is simply enjoying life with her husband and family. You can find and follow Gloria on FB: Gloria.Duckett1, IG @mrsgloriasfcc or christianmarriageetiquette@gmail.com

FOREWARD

In our society today, there are so many distractions that compete for attention among married couples that make marriage longevity look very bleak. Technology is at the forefront of most of our daily interactions. Our social lives are no longer centered on communication with our spouses and children. Today, many people go out not to socialize, but to share their "social experience." Today, consumers want experiences that they can share with their friends on social media and sometimes they forget to share these moments with their spouses.

Despite all these negative influences, Gloria and Dwayne Duckett's marriage has survived more than forty years and is still going strong. They even once led their church's marriage ministry. They have put in the work from a young to a seasoned couple and have together, accepted the challenges of marriage and have worked to find solutions and have never traded nor thrown their marriage away. They are certainly an example of commitment to the vows they made and continue to believe the best is yet to come.

Their relationship is based on God's word, which signifies that the husband and wife are like that of Christ and the Church. I believe they understand the scripture when Jesus said that marriage would go cold in the last days and people would no longer believe in the sanctity of it.

Today, many couples would rather live together rather than commit to marriage. Or, if you will, trade-in or trade-off like a used car if you wanted another one or a newer model. They are a committed couple who still wear a smile, laughing and wishing the best for their respective spouse by always being seen following the principles they are willing to be transparent about and share with you.

If you are a married couple and your marriage is great, they salute you. But, if you and your spouse's marriage is in trouble, I admonish you to bathe in the principles they share in this book, Christian Marriage Etiquette. Be ready to take off layers and undress when and where needed.

-Mary L. Green, PhD.

Associate Pastor, Membership Engagement
Bridge Builders International Church

ACKNOWLEDGEMENTS

To my wonderful husband, Dwayne Duckett:

Thank you for loving me from day one. Without you, there would not be a Christian Marriage Etiquette to share with the world. 40+ years down together... forever dedicated to learning and growing.

To my pastor, Dr. Johnasen L. Pack:

Eight years ago, you spoke into my life and it has been made better because of you. During your "The 8th Try" book signing, which is a national bestseller, you told me I was next; well, here I am!

To my dear friend, Libra P. Green:

Thank you for pushing me, encouraging me, and putting my dreams before your own to get my first book written and published. I could have gone another way, but God directed me to you.

To all readers: Thank you for purchasing and reading Christian Marriage Etiquette. You all were on my mind when I began writing my thoughts on paper. I hope you are blessed after reading Christian Marriage Etiquette and that your marriage will catch on fire and grow stronger.

CHRISTIAN MARRIAGE ETIQUETTE

12 Tips to Help Restore and Bring Balance to Your Marriage

By Gloria Duckett

Christian Marriage Etiquette   Gloria Duckett

INTRODUCTION

How many of you, regarding marriage, have ever asked or even told yourself, "If I only knew then what I know now?" You might have even said to yourself, "I wished someone would have told me this or that about marriage!"

I am here to tell you that it's not too late to start. If you are a divorcee, it's not too late to begin again. There are too many marriages heading to divorce court when it can be prevented if they know how to work on fixing simple things within their marriage. With over four decades of marriage, my husband and I have learned a few things along this journey called life, regardless of our upbringing. My parents divorced when I was two years old; my father never acknowledged us. People knew my father better than I did; he had another family that we didn't even know about, but others did.

Throughout life, you will have significant people to be a part of it, leaving their print in your heart. One of those significant people was my beloved grandmother, Rosie Lee. She was born on March 12th. She was a strong woman; as a pioneer, she had her vegetables canned and picked cotton in the field. She worked day in and day out to help put food on the table for her three children. She was a major role model in my life; one who equipped and trained me to become a strong woman, determined to make things work within the family. I am so much like her. I learned how to cook, quilt, sew, garden, and shoot a rifle.

When my stepfather, Mr. Alex Grant (we called him Mr. G) came into my mother's life, he loved and took care of her and us just the same. He was the best father I have ever known. She was a good wife and mother. God placed him in her life not only for her but to help provide and protect the family. There was never any form of disrespect on either part. They made it work until death parted them. They had a very Godly kind of marriage.

After forty years of marriage, we both are still committed to our covenant vows, which are built on the foundation of God's word while living a well-balanced life. Quitting is never an option for either one of us.

Upon reading this book, I want each reader to know and understand that marriage is not easy nor for the faint at heart, but it is well worth it. If you are a newlywed, have been married, or have a desire to be married, just know marriage takes work. Young couples, as well as old, will benefit from these great tips being shared within this book. I also want you to know that you're not alone. The smallest change for the better can make a big difference. There is hope for every marriage. You must want it bad enough without giving up.

OUR STORY

If there is such a thing as a "marriage manual," where was it when my husband and I needed it the most? Frankly, there isn't a concrete manual for marriage; however, my favorite book is filled with wisdom and principles to counsel and guide you along life's journey.

When my husband, Dwayne and I got married over forty years ago, neither one of us came into it with knowledge of what marriage was or its etiquette. I'll be transparent in sharing some of our lessons learned regarding marriage within the book. Neither one of us had good examples of married couples around us in our lives that honored their covenant vows to each other for a long period. Honestly, there were people around us that grew up in homes where proper etiquette and good manners didn't exist.

In my upbringing, we both saw our parents struggling within their marriage because they did not know how to treat each other. As adults, we both found out within our marriage that we just didn't know what we didn't know. We went into our marriage with those same unlearned habits and behaviors that were passed down to us, learning quickly that it can and will destroy a marriage.

We were never given a "marriage manual" to go along with our marriage license. When we got married, we made a covenant vow before God to step over the threshold anyway and grow through it. You shouldn't enter a marriage with a mindset that you cannot try to change your spouse. We both worked tirelessly to learn and grow in our strengths and weaknesses and each other, which is key in sustaining a healthy marriage.

Christian Marriage Etiquette Gloria Duckett

We must respect ourselves and each other's differences; if not, it could create barriers within the marriage quickly.

Every married couple must be willing to put in the hard work it takes to make a marriage work 24/7, 365 days a year. To witness younger generations view marriage as it is shown on social media platforms, including television and film is a sad reality. The deception to believe everything within the marriage is "perfect" and all well put together based on what they see often from media outlets, is far from the truth.

I believe without our younger generations being properly taught, conditioned, and/or educated about the expectations, roles, and responsibilities of marriage, they will go into it blindsided, simply because of the false pretense and/or an illusion of what a marriage will look like. A few months into the marriage, they will soon discover that it is not the case.

What you watch (on television and/or film), may not be the same for you after you say your vows. Who you thought was the right one (for you) may end up being the total opposite for you when in reality, they were the wrong one since day one. You want to make sure that the person you are married to/marrying is solely based on the facts about them, not the fantasies regarding them.

As such things in life change, it occurs even in marriages, as well. Whether a couple has been married a year or even five years, life will bring about a change. The once young and vibrant spouse will become a much lesser vibrant spouse. One day, you're on top of the clouds; the next, you're ready to walk out the door. The times are changing when it comes to marriage. The world has even tried to change the definition of marriage; however, marriage is not a union if it was not ordained by God.

Christian Marriage Etiquette — Gloria Duckett

Marriage is about loving, honoring, and respecting each other. When the love, respect, and honor are gone, the foundation of the marriage is greatly challenged. Sadly, we often hear of marriages today as a means of convenience and/or for purposes to have all the "legal" sex you want. The disheartening thing is when the long-lasting covenant or commitment to neither God nor each other is no longer present; they are ready to head to divorce court.

There aren't many models of seasoned married couples being presented in the forefront in this day and age, leaving a vast number of couples with a lack of knowledge of knowing what a real marriage is like. Without a healthy model to observe and/or follow, the lack of displaying real love and marriage will continue to evolve.

Wholeheartedly, I believe this is the very thing they need, because they have not seen married couples staying married and strong in it for ten years or longer. Although I was raised around many failed and/or unhappily married couples in my era, I chose to be happy in my marriage; it has been one of the best decisions I have made in my life.

As I mentioned before, in the era I grew up in when a man and a woman got married, most of them were the "till death do us part" kind of marriage. Regardless of what took place or what was happening in the marriage, they chose to stay together; however, most of them weren't happy or fulfilled with one another. The covenant vow made before God was what they held onto, but like anything else, some still chose to just walk away without putting in the work.

When my husband and I got married, our motto was and remains to be "if we can't fit together or if God can't fix it, then

Christian Marriage Etiquette — Gloria Duckett

it can't be fixed." As a happily married woman, my husband and I both want to help you make your marriage become a loving and lasting one, becoming the "to death do us part" kind of marriage. If you both implement these tips the right way, the solutions will come quickly. Let's get to work! You can thank Dwayne and me later.

Let us first take a moment to share our story with you. As an unapologetic Christian, we live our life according to the word and principles of God, according to scripture. Dwayne and I grew up together in a small town in Texas but didn't know each other. One night, I met him at church; he was 21 and I was 18.

Neither one of us wanted to go but went anyway. I only went to church because of my grandmother; she lived down the street from the church but on this night, I had to take her. Dwayne was supposed to be playing the guitar for his brother as he preached but he came to church "looking for the ladies." He told his sister there were "no ladies up in there." His sister told him, "Yes, there are! Gloria is in there." He looked through the window and later, came into the church. Child, I never paid him any attention. I didn't have time for that.

After church service, he was waiting on the outside of the church doors. He said, "Hey, can I get your number?" My initial thought was, "Really! Boy that was fast," but I didn't want my grandmother to see me talking to some guy so, I kindly said to him, "No, I already have your number," and I moved on. His sister was trying to get with my brother during that time, so I didn't call him… until later. When I finally did, his sister told me he had joined the Army; after that night, I did not ask anyone about him.

Christian Marriage Etiquette   Gloria Duckett

It wasn't until my senior year in high school when I got in contact with Dwayne, my "Pen Pal." During this moment of my life, I was in an unstable relationship and pregnant by my childhood boyfriend, whom I have grown up with and had known since we were toddlers. To be honest, my senior year was a very rough year for me. My mother had a heart attack and had to have bypass heart surgery and was in recovery with my grandmother.

All of this was happening while I was getting ready to graduate. Before that, I was ready to quit school. I was ready to leave the state and start over with my new baby, but where was I going to go? I had no clue, but God had a better plan for my life. I just needed someone to talk to... just to get me through my senior year in high school. Somehow, I got a hold of Dwayne's sister and got his mailing address.

I planned to only become pen pals with him, so I wrote him a letter or two and sent him my graduation photos. That's how we began to start writing to each other. God communicates and deals with me in dreams, so one night, I dreamed that I married a man wearing all Army green. In one of his letters, he said he was coming home in June to visit his mother, whose birthday was June 1st, which was good to know. During his visit home, there was a church service taking place and his brother was preaching at this service. The phone rings. "Hello, can I speak to Gloria?!" "This is she." "Hey, can I come to see you?" "Who is this?!" "Dwayne." "What?!" I was shocked but I said, "Sure, come on down."

Anyone who knows my husband knows he has this distinction about himself. As he walks into the house, immediately I tell him to sit on the other side of the couch while I sit across from him. The reason why I had him sit on the other side was because there was a mirror in the hallway and my grandmother sees anyone sitting on the couch; that was too funny! He wanted me to sit by him, but no sir; that wasn't going to happen. At this time in my life, I was four months pregnant with another guy's baby. Dwayne didn't know my pregnancy until he saw me in person during the visit. It was never mentioned in my letters to him because I was only writing him as a "Pen Pal."

We were having a conversation for a while and out of nowhere, he pops the question, "Do you want to get married?" Now mind you, I'm pregnant by a person who kept denying the child was his own until after her birth, but that's another story. I knew this was in God's plan because of the dream I had. Without hesitation, I simply said, "Sure." We were married on the 14th of June and the rest is history; four decades later, we're still going strong.

Many said we would not make it, but we have seen the naysayers go through three or four marriages. We never had any marriage etiquette training or marriage counseling before nor during our marriage. I am stating that marriage counseling isn't strongly recommended and/ or needed for your marriage. Just know and understand when you know it is God, it will work. Yes, it will take work, but it can and will work if you work it.

If anyone has been through it or has done it, we have been there. We didn't want the t-shirt or coffee mug. When we have an issue, we bounce back quickly because of the foundation we place our marriage upon, which is the Word of God and you can too. We have gone through the fire and the rain, yet by God's grace and mercy we both know for sure He will carry us through.

Christian Marriage Etiquette Gloria Duckett

As you've read, you noticed my husband and I never dated; we got married on the fly for real, for real. Vividly, I still remember one of his aunts peeking in the bedroom of his mother's house on our honeymoon. I looked up wondering "what in the world are they coming in here for?". She told me "Stay with him honey; follow him wherever he goes!" And that is exactly what I did; however, let me be honest. My favorite book says in Proverbs 18:22, "He who finds a wife, finds a good thing". And He did! We have never been apart for a long time. The longest we have ever been apart was when he changed duty stations.

Our first year was crazy! My life was accelerating quickly. I had just graduated, got married, and had a beautiful baby girl, getting ready to start my life as a wife and a mother. My husband was stationed in Savannah, Georgia at Hunter Army Airfield. Thankfully, he found a place to rent right outside of the gate. You see, do not get married if your husband does not have a home for his bride. I was still at home but one of the hardest decisions that I had to ever make in my life was to leave my baby girl at home with my mother for two heartfelt reasons: My mother had recently had a heart attack before our move. In my mind, I felt if I took my daughter away from my mother during that time, I would have lost my mother. The other reason is that I love my baby girl, however, I knew God had His reasons and knew what was best.

Within a whole year, I graduated high school, got married to a man that I barely knew anything about, and had my baby girl shortly after I had my daughter; I became pregnant again with our son while striving to adjust to being away from home and my daughter. Since my husband lived with his parents, his mother loved church and God; I figured he couldn't be all that bad and I was right. I was not an Army wife!

Christian Marriage Etiquette   Gloria Duckett

We got a chance to travel all over the world. As an Army wife, we had to learn how to sacrifice, mainly our time together. I was never a clingy, needy person. So, I was okay with it. He knew where home was and who was waiting at home for him. An old Army saying is, "The Army did not issue a wife". He was most definitely Army and I was a wife. However, Army was my life. The Army was all I knew. For the sake of my family, I placed my life on hold to support my husband get where he needed to be in the military ranks while staying at home to take care of our son and my second daughter whom we had a couple of years later. I knew what I had to do for my husband and children. Life was good and exciting all at the same time. I just had to trust the plan of God through it all. Through my own experiences, I choose to be an example of a happily married person to many individuals who are or desire to be married.

Even though my oldest daughter was with my mother (her grandmother), my mother never failed to communicate with me. Just like I made sure she always knew who her father was. My husband loved me and he loved my daughter as well. He gave her his last name. When I think about it, this is kind of like the story of Mary and Joseph. Wow! God is good and He's faithful. The plan He has for our lives is much more than what we can plan. My daughter has grown into a wonderful woman and mother. I see so much of myself in her. I tell her that I love her often, letting her know that I am there for her whenever she needs me. Just to be part of her life means so much to me.

For the most part, staying at home was fun. The only thing was that my daughter was not there to enjoy the journeys that my other two children had. But, as I stated earlier, God always knows what is best. We may have given birth to them, but may not raise them. She was in a good place. I never question what

Christian Marriage Etiquette   Gloria Duckett

God is doing, just know that He makes no mistakes. I have no regrets at all. I just knew what God required of me, regardless of the tough decisions I had to make.

We learned that there is no perfect person in life, but we know who is perfect in our eyes. We married our spouse with their flaws, faults, failures, fragilities, and all yet we must learn daily to give grace to all who God has granted His grace to.

We have had many ups and downs, trials, and tribulations throughout our marriage, but we always bounce back because of the foundation we place our marriage upon, which is the Word of God and you can too. We have gone through the fire and the rain, yet by God's grace and mercy, we both know He will carry us through.

With this being said, let's begin with Christian Marriage Etiquette. I honor my beloved husband for his role and responsibility in producing these tips with you in mind. It is my prayer along with my husband's, that you have an open mindset and heart, allowing God to speak directly to you and your "now moment."

So, are you ready? Come along the journey with my husband and me as we both share some tips that continue to keep us together.

CHRISTIAN MARRIAGE ETIQUETTE
12 TIPS TO HELP RESTORE AND BRING BALANCE BACK TO YOUR MARRIAGE

TIP #1

Marriage is a work in progress. If you want to keep peace in your home, keep other people out of your business.

The worst thing you can do in your marriage is put your business in the ears of other people. Many people do want to see you prosper; however, some want you both to break up so you can be with them. Allow me to help you: your business is your business!

If you feel there is a need to talk to someone outside of your marriage, make it your intent for both of you to talk to your pastor or a professional counselor. To talk to your "girls" or your "boys" about your marriage problems will cause friction within your home; in time, they will become vultures, waiting for the marriage to crumble.

Proverbs 16:28 states, "A dishonest man spreads strife, and a whisperer separates close friends."

Even though you want to share what is going on in your marriage with your close friends, please don't. The life of your marriage depends on it. The person you should communicate with is the person you are a covenant with, which is your spouse.

TIP #2

When things get rough, do not go back to the familiar.

When you disagree, deal with, and resolve it right away. The longer it takes to resolve an issue, the easier it is for you to go back to the familiar to cope. Yes, we all have our different coping mechanisms, but are they healthy?

Many times, people go back to or become exposed to drinking, smoking, or even an ex or a new person. Your mind begins to play tricks on you. You'll start hearing thoughts in your head like, "Maybe I shouldn't have married him" or "I need to go back to my ex; at least they understand me." These are some of the lies used to break up what God has ordained. Learn to work things out with each other.

Communication is the key to any successful and happy marriage. Take a moment to process, breathe, cool down, but fix it quickly as possible. When things get rough, work it out!

TIP #3

Flowers are okay now and then. But you must give them "something" they can feel all the time.

We love flowers and gifts; however, flowers and gifts are good now and then, but your spouse needs "something" they can feel all the time. This means you must provide some kind of physical touch or intimacy all of the time. This could be a 30-second kiss, a lasting hug, or a quickie during lunch. Intimacy is not just about sex but we all know men are sexual beings; women are more emotional beings.

Find balance to satisfy and meet the needs of your spouse all the time. So, you may need to bring some flowers or a screwdriver some time, just make sure you bring them something they can feel. Marriage is all about being and staying connected with your spouse as one. Connection is essential to marriage and to have it with your spouse is different from the connection with a friend.

TIP #4

Sports are back! You can love it, sit down, and pretend to like it or we can start a new hobby... just do not catch a case!

It has been known that the number of cases of domestic violence normally rises when it is sports season. Some women like sports; some don't at all. Many women feel left out when the spouse is absorbed by the game. This is a good time for the spouse to find a hobby, go shopping or simply sit down and learn the game for you, men and/or women.

Men love it when their spouses become interested in something that they like to do. You just do not want to catch a case from being in your feelings for a few hours. He will probably give you money just for you to leave. Let them have and enjoy their moment. They will be back to themselves after the game. Just be loving and ready.

Proverbs 14:1 says "The wisest of women builds her house, but folly with her own hands tears it down."

A wise woman will let her husband do his thing while she finds something else to occupy her time until after the sporting event.

A good idea is to create a sports wives Facebook group page to communicate with other wives. You noticed that I said "wives." Married women should hang out with married women. It is the same thing with married men. This group could be a good place to meet and connect with others during game times.

Make sure your spouse is good before leaving; most importantly, let your spouse know what you are doing. We don't want to have nor create any more issues to attack the marriage. Kiss your spouse and be on your way for the next few hours with the ladies. Oh, don't forget his credit card.

TIP #5

Love is... forgiving your spouse regardless of their past, present, and future. It all began when you said, "I do".

Before you said, "I do," you accepted your spouse with their flaws and all. When you say, "I do," it means you agreed to take on the good, the bad, and the ugly after the vows daily. When you said, "I do," it meant you forgave them for all they did before the marriage and become willing to forgive each other during the marriage. You cannot go into marriage thinking that you can change your spouse. They are who they are. The only person you can change with the help of the good Lord is you. You do not want to live in a controlling marriage, but a loving and lasting one.

We are all human and we are going to make mistakes; however, we must be careful of what we do and how we do it for the sake of not causing harm or defiling the marriage. When we mess up, own it by being responsible but forgive and recover quickly. You cannot bring up the past when you get married for it will only cause friction and division between both of you, when you are to remain unified as one.

Focus on the good things while looking forward to a wonderful present and future with each other. Forgive, let it go, and move forward together! The past is called the past for a reason. That's why it is important to lay it all on the line before you take the vows. You do not want to be shocked when some hidden stuff comes out during a heated dispute.

TIP #6

Give him what he wants... give her what she needs.

Whew, Honey Child! I promise this tip will keep you out of divorce court! My husband and I have taught each other so much over the years. Oh, my goodness, we are still learning! Mind you, we didn't know each other at all. He knew my father and grandparents but did not know that I existed. He's an introvert and I am an extrovert (that's a whole other story too!). He didn't talk very much and I'm like the energizer bunny. To ask him any closed-ended questions is like pulling teeth from a chicken.

When it comes to love languages, his love language is words of affirmation; mine is acts of service. If you have read the book by Gary Chapman, "The Five Love Languages," I strongly recommend that you both take a moment to read it from beginning to end. In our marriage, he wants me to tell him how great he is and how much I need him. It doesn't matter how many gifts I buy him, which he loves, but if I don't communicate in his love language, then I am not meeting his needs. The same applies to me as well; I love to see him doing things for me (especially mowing the lawn shirtless) and doing things for me without me asking. Yes, he tells me how great I am too but if he doesn't communicate with me in the same regard as I do with him, there is friction.

Remember, marriage is a give/give union with a 100% investment into it... not a give and take. Your assignment is to be the rest of the other one. Other than that, each could have done it on their own before marriage. Marriage isn't covenanted to take away from each other's emotional, mental, spiritual, and physical bank. You are an asset... a compliment to one another.

It is important to build one another to remain as one because if you don't, in time they will look or even get it from someone else. The old-timers used to say, "When you say, 'Scat cat', somebody else will say, 'Here kitty, kitty.'" You want to find ways to meet in the middle. Some things your spouse may or may not feel comfortable doing, but, "no" is not an option in marriage. Be open to find creative ways to keep your spouse wanting more.

This is where balance within the marriage comes in. The divorce rate among Christians is just as high as the divorce rate as non-Christians. Why? There is no balance within the marriage. If you spend all of your time in church, then your spouse is missing out at home. You can't be in the spirit all the time; you need to satisfy your spouse physically, intimately, and if at all possible, sexually. Wives give it up to your husbands. You might be thinking he's looking at you, but he's looking at that little honey behind you. Never give the other one eye to wander.

Here's a tip for free, between you and your spouse, there are no limits in the bedroom. My favorite book says in 1 Corinthians 7:4, the wife gives authority over her body to her husband, and the husband gives authority over his body to his wife. Marriage is a give/give union. Let's avoid divorce court and learn what your spouse's needs and wants are. Be open to explore and create "new normals."

Tip #7

Marriage is not for the immature.

Marriage is great for the young at heart. But it can be a disaster waiting to happen when you are not ready. When my husband and I got married, he was 21 and I was 18, which is known to be fairly young. Although our marriage thrived from a young age, it is discovered that most marriages do not last long when you marry young. Some of the reason is that neither person knows what they want at that time and/or they may be trying to figure out who they are as a person. When this happens, eventually, they will let the marriage die out of unrealistic expectations than when they came into the marriage. They did not expect all the pressure, commitments, quality time, along with all the bills and problems that come with the "I do." Before you enter into a covenant of marriage, you must count the costs and be ready to endure the good, the bad, and the ugly... together.

There will be some things about a person that you didn't see beforehand and vice versa and now it arises during the marriage. Marriages will have little spats; however, it isn't a definite reason to take your ball home once you put a ring on them. Some people will let you see what they want you to see, but with your spouse, there is no exception. You're no longer in high school. You must grow in maturity and you are both now living a married life. There is no "running home to mommy and daddy" when the toilet paper is not put back on the holder or the toilet seat was left up. My favorite book states in Matthew 19:5, "And he said, 'For this reason, a man will leave his father and mother and be united to his wife and the two will become one.'" There may be a moment or two where you must return home, but if this happens, it shouldn't be for a long time.

Here is another thing to consider in regards to maturity. You must know each other's friends and enemies, especially if it is a new marriage. It is not the time to become neither jealous nor envious; remember they had friends and exes before you. You will have to be mature about creating and setting safe boundaries in your marriage by having conversations when needed. If a spouse feels some type of way about a friendship or association their spouse is in, it is NOT the moment or opportunity to place your love in an awkward situation. If they wanted their ex, they would have married them, yet they chose you to be their spouse. Most importantly, this is when you want to work on self-improvement because a mature marriage will last a lifetime.

TIP # 8

Express your love to your spouse every day.

Do not wait to get in front of people to express your love to your spouse. Develop some effective ways to express your love to your spouse, including in private. I have learned what you do in private, it is naturally shown in public. Learn to be active and open to express your love every day, whether it's at home, work, church, or even on the street.

You can express your love in many ways. You can express your love by running a bubble bath, giving them a massage, a romantic candlelight dinner with a bottle of their favorite wine, or giving them a gift card to their favorite place. You do not have to display open affection to one another, especially when it is not appropriate. You want to always be considerate and respectful with your spouse.

Most importantly, respect your spouse. People can clearly see and tell how much you love your spouse through your actions, thoughts, or deeds. Don't be a freak at home and put on your "halo" when you get in public. Be consistent! Don't start and then stop! It's okay to let the world know you have the best spouse in the world. Some people may not be comfortable displaying their affection openly and that is okay.

Christian Marriage Etiquette   Gloria Duckett

You can still express your love to your spouse, simply by holding hands or by giving a kiss on the cheek. If you love each other, do not be ashamed to express it. Have fun! Enjoy the journey... together.

TIP #9

A healthy marriage will have disputes and heated discussions.

From time to time, a healthy marriage will have disputes or heated discussions. This is a good thing because having them from time to time means you're still willing to fight fair without becoming verbally, emotionally, or physically abusive within the marriage. Every marriage will have arguments and disagreements. It is when you no longer choose to fight fair, your marriage is headed to a marriage counselor or even worse, divorce court.

Healthy disputes and disagreements once resolved can often lead to foreplay, that's if you are creative and put in the work. The "making up" is always fun for my husband and me and it can be for you as well. A married couple can fight fair by taking time to actively listen to one another before speaking. You both must ensure what you're trying to convey is clear, concise, and heard correctly. To go back and forth or playing tit for tat with each other will only make matters worse.

Take a moment to listen and hear each other out and get an understanding, even if you must agree to disagree sometimes. When we had heated discussions or disagreements, our children never heard us yell nor raise our voices. We took it to our bedroom and talked about it like adults. Your problems should not become your children's problems. Work things out and keep fighting fair; your marriage depends on it.

TIP #10

You are not in competition with each other but to complete each other.

Over the years, I have seen many married couples in competition with one other. This is unhealthy and if you aren't careful, it will cause problems within the marriage. It doesn't matter how much money one makes over the other.

When you get married, you must already know your assignment or role within the marriage. Therefore, it is important to have healthy conversations often. You want to sit down and decide who will do what. For example, find out who will pay the mortgage and who will pay the utilities. Whichever way the decision may be, you both are in this marriage together as one. Learn and grow together as one, being open to being the rest of each other. It is no longer "my money" or "your money" it has become "our money" You are trying to build a home and eventually a family together. Do not tear it down before it begins.

Remember, marriage is a give and give, not a give and take. Wives, your assignment is to help him as the priest of your home. As the head of your household, when he looks good as the representation of your home, you both look good. When you become one, there will be no time for anything else but to completely love each other as Christ loves us. The only time to compete with each other is trying to out love each other. Have fun!

TIP #11

Watch out for "That Thang!"

When your past tries to call you back, be careful. As a matter of fact, run in the opposite direction as fast as you can, especially when it begins to feel comfortable enough to call back. We all know what "that thing" is in your life: your ex. The enemy will come to you, attempting to make sure you are standing on your vows, "I do."

The enemy knows exactly when you're feeling "some kind of way" and/or you are being in your emotions about your marriage. One of the ways you know when "that thing" is trying to destroy and/or come against your marriage is when you get a call out of nowhere (delete the number!) or out of nowhere, you run into them at the store. The spirit of familiarity will always show up, but your job is to recognize it without entertaining the idea or thought. "That thing" will not take out time to just show up in your life, as if they did not know God had plans for you and your marriage. We're never tempted with something we do not love, but it is always something that gets the fire burning in us. Many great men and women have fallen prey to "that thing".

My favorite book says in Deuteronomy 32:20, "one can chase a thousand devils and two can chase two thousand." So, you see how powerful a marriage ordained by God is? As a wife of a military veteran, I have seen many families destroyed because one person decided to go back to 'that thing' which made them comfortable.

Some marriages I have observed over the years were destroyed because of the fear of being abandoned or afraid of becoming a widow or widower, especially during Desert Storm/Desert Shield. There was so much infidelity going on during the war and at home. Wives were breaking down, unable to deal with their husbands being away from the family. It was awful! But, I kept the faith all while trying to help wives deal with depression.

Take heart and do not be deceived; whatever "that thing" was from your past, it will raise its ugly head up to destroy your marriage. That thing isn't identified just as a person; it could be pornography, gambling, drugs, alcohol, your job, family, or even old friends; the list is endless. The most vulnerable part of your marriage is where "that thing" will show up. Do not give anyone or anything any play that will cause your marriage to crumble. I promise you, it is not worth it.

You and only you know exactly what "that thing" is in your life. When you find yourself in that situation, shut it down quickly and give no space to it; do not entertain it for one second. Stand strong in your marriage and fight for it. Just remember, you married each other until death do you both part.

TIP # 12

Keep the home fires burning!

A boring, unfilled marriage is at high risk for infidelity unless things change within the marriage. Normally, if a marriage is boring and/or unfilled, there is a deficiency somewhere that needs to be addressed. The old-timers used to say, "An idle mind is the devil's workshop. When your spouse gets bored, the mind and eye will begin to wander.

As an individual, it is important to work on yourself from time to time regarding self-care. Make sure you're healthy both physically and mentally. Remember, men are visual and women are emotional. You want to be able to take care of what you need to take care of when the time comes. Keeping the fire and passion alive within your marriage will help keep the spouse from seeking and finding it outside the home. Whatever you were doing before your marriage, you must do just as much, if not twice as much to maintain it.

Many marriages begin to get cold after a while for several reasons. There is no such thing as "falling out of love." Marriages can lose their fire due to stress, bills, work, ministry, children, and/or even medical reasons. Whatever it is, you must keep the passion and fire in your marriage. If not, just know that there are many "vultures" waiting in the wings with a match ready to strike it.

A spark can be something simple as a thought or stroke behind the ear with a soft, gentle finger. Take a walk back down memory lane. Let your mind go back to that first night when your eyes connected across the room. I promise you when you let go of the hustle and grinds of life and think about the most important thing in life, which is your spouse and marriage, things will work out for the best. Always keep that spark for the love of your life for the rest of your lives.

With all of that, let's have some fun. We have added a Fondness and Admiration Questionnaire for you and your spouse.

FONDNESS AND ADMIRATION QUESTIONNAIRE

Answer the following true or false questions.

1. I can easily list the three things I most admire about my partner. **T or F**
2. When we are apart, I often think fondly of my partner. **T or F**
3. I will often find some way to tell my partner "I love you." **T or F**
4. I often touch or kiss my partner affectionately. **T or F**
5. My partner really respects me. **T or F**
6. I feel loved and cared for in this relationship. **T or F**
7. I feel accepted and liked by my partner. **T or F**
8. My partner finds me sexy and attractive. **T or F**
9. My partner turns me on sexually. **T or F**
10. There is a fire and passion in this relationship. **T or F**
11. Romance is still a part of our relationship. **T or F**
12. I am proud of my partner. **T or F**
13. My partner really enjoys my achievements and accomplishments. **T or F**
14. I can easily tell you why I want to marry my partner. **T or F**
15. If I had it all to do over again, I would. **T or F**
16. We rarely part from each other without showing some sign of love and affection. **T or F**
17. When I come into a room, my partner is glad to see me. **T or F**

18. My partner appreciates the things I do in this relationship. **T or F**
19. My spouse generally likes my personality. **T or F**
20. Our life is generally satisfying. **T or F**

Scoring 10 or above is good. 10 or below shows room for improvements.

CLOSING THOUGHTS

Wow! That's all we have right now. These are just a few of the Christian Marriage Etiquette tips. There is so much more to explore! My husband and I wanted you to be knowledgeable and informed that marriage will work if you work it. No one is perfect; the only perfect One is the One who has ordained marriage since the foundation of the world. My Pastor Dr. Johnasen L. Pack said "Before marriage, there has to be a funeral. Both of you must die at the altar." When you both die to your own flesh, you then can truly live as one, bone of his bone and flesh of his flesh. Enjoy your lives together, love each other, and do not allow anyone or anything to come between what God has joined together.

Will every day be a day of bliss or sunshine? No. There will be times in your marriage when you just want to give it up and go live on a chicken farm (a little humor there). When thoughts of stepping out of your marriage, divorce or other feelings come to your mind, quickly remove them with positive reinforcements. Know and understand daily your why: why did you get married? It is only a test to see if you meant your vows, one to another.

Also, look at marriage like having a lifetime gym membership. Just because you have a gym membership does not mean you will automatically build strength or muscle. You will need to work out consistently. You must be physically, emotionally, and spiritually ready and the more you work on your marriage, the stronger your marriage will become. When obstacles come your way, keep moving forward... together.

Fall in love again and be each other's friend. There are times you might not need your spouse, but you will need the friend within your spouse. It only takes a memory but always remember when, how, and why you fell in love. Your love for each other can and will endure a lifetime, just the way God intended. Fall in love with yourself first; it is hard to love others until you first love yourself.

When you build your marriage on the solid foundation of God, there is nothing in this world or the world itself that can shake it. Feel free to reach out to my husband and me. We will keep it real with you. We want your marriage to endure until the end.

Grace and Peace to you both!

REFERENCES

Chapman, Gary D. The Five Love Languages. Walker Large Print, 2010.

Scripture quotations marked KJV are taken from the Holy Bible, King James Version.

Gottman, John and Nan Silver: The Seven Principles For Making Marriage Work: A Practical Guide From the Country's Foremost Relationship Expert (New York: Three Rivers Press, 1999)

www.ingramcontent.com/pod-product-compliance
Lightning Source LLC
Chambersburg PA
CBHW050707160426
43194CB00010B/2045